Handling Filth:
Simple Sabotage Field Manual

Jared Schickling

Unlikely Books
www.UnlikelyStories.org
New Orleans, Louisiana

ISBN: 979-8-9851371-9-4

Library of Congress Control Number: 2022942347

Unlikely Books
www.UnlikelyStories.org
New Orleans, Louisiana

Handling Filth:

Simple Sabotage Field Manual

The Order in Which They Appear

Infection   9
Simple Sabotage Field Manual   23
Automobiles in Quarantine   45
Data Befall Alibi   63
Reports   71

Acknowledgments   93
About the Author   94
Other Books by Jared Schickling   95
Recent Titles from Unlikely Books   96

repulsed by real
as it is by real
imagine
noble tool

      B and P, it was this

Infection

On That Day My Soul Grew Smells

Once upon a midnight infection
—tormentor of my dreams
When I think of it
as I lay, engaged and contaminating, and awoke

I awoke and flung the infestation
That seizure became the lonely sepsis
"Infection!" chuckled I "Yes infection!" later, soon [1]
new dreams became, animal bite

---

[1] After an unconfirmed bout of the vid in January of 2020 lays low the ██████'s family, and wanting a cigarette, the repetend apes the refrain during Summer's song in Thomas Nashe's English comedy, *Summer's Last Will and Testament*, performed in London in 1592 while theaters were closing: "I am sick, I must die." Anthologized today as "A Litany in Time of Plague," the personified Summer, introduced to the audience by Will Summer, being Will Sommers, or Somers, Will Somer, no one really knows, Henry VIII's favorite court jester, sings of a pestilence arrived from Earth to devour life and hope, leaving the voice to despair of "fate," in "what vain art can reply."

Infamous infections, however hard they try, will [2]
always be amazing.
Irritating, irresponsible, infamous infections.
Are you upset by how astonishing they are? Does it tear
you apart to see the infamous infections so awful?

I saw the amazing diseases of lost generations destroyed,
how I mourned the superficial sepsis.
But now, did it make you shiver?
do they?

Pay attention to the initial infestation,
the initial infestation—the most fat fullness of it all.

is this that makes me
stay inside, shiver?

---

[2] World media is reporting that a reincarnation of Henry VIII has revealed itself, wearing musty, orange skin and occupying a gold-plated throne inside the American Empire.

Deep into that darkness sneezing, once upon a midnight smell
of "Cough!" said I, "thing of three."
I sat engaged and vomiting.

Gut turned tussal hemoptysis
And on that day my bed grew sappy.
Cough—tormentor of my dreams.

Our Quarantine Course, Your Office Be the Best.

        ease, however hard I try,

Will always be tricky.
Degenerative, digestive,
ease. Down, down, down into the darkness of the
ease. Gently they go, gone, beyond the window—the awe-inspiring, the awful, the awesome.

Pay attention to the serious sepsis, with beer
unemployed serious sepsis is the most amazing infection of it all.
So, ease is just the thing
To get me wondering if serious sepsis, beyond the window, is awful?

Beyond the window, initial infestation became, in its way.
An initial infestation gets wooly-   an initial infestation gets
an intestinal infestation gets muddled, however.

I cannot help but stop and look at severe immunodeficiency.
The ease. Are you upset by how serious it is?
Does it tear you apart to see the immunodeficiency so dangerous?

Citizens, however hard they try,

what is that
in there?

"Cough!" chuckled I "Yes cough!"
how I flung some spit
as passions became my decongestant
I'd seen their colds near [3]

---

[3] As the infected are reporting a loss of smell before feeling sick, by April of 2020, the American news cycle is mired in baseless claims that a newly identified, novel coranvirus may be no worse than the seasonal flu. Eight months later, at the end of the year, after a 15.9% increase in the age-adjusted mortality rate, the Center for Disease Control and Prevention (CDC) attributes 377,883 deaths to COVID-19 in the U.S. alone.

a potter's field cough—tormentor of my dreams.
Once upon a midnight rrhea
"Cough!" said I, "thing of catarrh."
A plaque would be laid in their sternutative
grasses, in nature's sternutative
vomit, deep into that darkness
gulping "Cough!" chuckled I "Yes cough!" but I
would awake and fleer at these sternutations.
And so I knew the headache
the tussal, sneezy sniffling.
Once I lay engaged and smelling
of nothing, and on that day my soul grew congested.

The Strange and Amazing Infection
an auto-generated American poem

Whose infection is that? I think I know.
Its owner is quite happy, though.
Full of joy, like a vivid rainbow,
I watch him laugh. I cry hello.

He gives his infection a shake,
And coughs until his belly aches.
The only other sound's the break
Of distant waves, and markets awake.

The infection is strange, amazing and deep,
But he has promises to keep,
After cake and induced sleep,
Sweet dreams come to him cheap.

He rises from his gentle bed,
With thoughts of productivity in his head,
He eats his brains with lots of bread,
Gets ready for the day ahead.

Infection of the breath, and all the sea
This anguish of earth.

My own infection, and the winds of the sea
My words have fared to their promise.

This infection, of the wind, coasting
Visualized are the silent easts, and the forests [4]

That infection has come to thoughts,
In a word, it came

An infection of the mist, in me
This transmission of years with the sound of the sea.

---

[4] The off-color ███████ appears in January, on the lips of a strangely cruel, orange-colored American president. By April, researchers across the planet are studying the pandemic's transmission mechanism through breath.

For in a Kingdom Full of Fevers

Once upon a midnight decongestant
When much I marveled the rrhea trench mouth
It left me lonely, sneezy, wheezing.
"Cough!" said I, "thing of wheeze."
"Cough!" chuckled I "Yes cough!"
Shall I do the cough
Cough—tormentor of my dreams
I still marvel the congestant mucus
Once I sat engaged and spitting
Once upon a midnight rrhea
When I think of the cough
And passion became the antipyretic squirt
On that day my soul grew silent.
I awoke and seeped in it, like some flue
Deep into that darkness gargling.
Once upon a midnight disinfectant
I sat engaged and bleaching
In a kingdom full of handwashes
How I'd pour today the happy mercurochrome,
T'was passion then such freezable deodorizer, to have but
Awoken with some activated charcoal
For graves, you see, you accept placebos
After the zinc is gone.

Traveling through, I
The glass was kept full, the kids are
There wasn't much to do with each other, for
I hadn't been outside since
Went into effect
There's a knock on my door but I
It was a test, is what I've

How happy is the severe immunodeficiency!
Are you upset by how austere it is?
Did it tear you apart to see the immunodeficiency so plain?

Lung fogs the glass for
The news, out the window
"lung glass," made you shiver?
What is that, in there?

something stinks in here, there's the window
PASSION BECAME THE LONELY TOWELETTE

And then one day, my days grew splendid
I awoke and flung the hypochlorite
In a kingdom full of swabs luck
Hope I smelled a lonely, detergent soaping

rattling

Our quarantined dance with our sky, and the storms,
a cancelation of the sea, shall we speak the sound.

Your quarantined hands once on our hills,
this simple passionate strength of the spring.

Your quarantined colors streamed from the wild grass,
a hope has come. And the day is mine

The quarantined marble, our flowers seem,
this lie in the sunlight, the palace.

A quarantined man in the calm waters of his throne,
his desire dies, and the blossoms.

Simple Sabotage Field Manual

in the key of C

Simple Sabotage Field Manual [1]

communication facility coffee cup polyester blend wire fire industrial production jerkey oil
corn lubrication runoff iron filing smelt dust fine sand ground glass chewing gum emery dust
cooling system refined water urine juice motor transformer wet wipe turbine boiler sand blast
aluminum can mine mineral extraction train car agriculture machinery crop livestock plastic
airport baggage vending machine switch tea bag signal routing water fountain road bed street
salt brake burger menstrual product vehicle cigarette butt battery pill shell ignition mustard
gear tire radiator grease shirt bottle navigation streetlight baby formula glitter binkie soap
lotion cola fleece barge cargoe stamp rubber coating transmission line
as microplastics began to appear
in arctic samples and human placentas

just another day, adapting
moody and dim, yet bright

plague—
happier squirrels and

song moving   like shadows
simple song in the moving,   shadows
of

         shadows of course
                  having been built
with happy thoughts in mind

who leaves this plaza of broken glass to the field now, this crumbling parking lot
even a penny had more sense there, in the pines, listen, so
remember, when you get there
lead with some sugar

who knew
it could breed and coo
and think and spread
toxic goo from a tree
through its hair to fell an elephant

---

[1] The Central Intelligence Agency's (CIA) "Simple Sabotage Field Manual" (Office of Strategic Services, 1944) informs anyone from highly trained operatives to high school discontents on how easy it is to sabotage a nation's wartime efforts. The poem titles correspond to the declassified, widely available, American manual's body headers, plus a quotation.

Under the Direction of Strategic Services

plastic sunk to dirt, a different part of it, shade
the plastic tocsin nicks the soul, at the time of asphyxiation
plastic animation, draft an envoy of what happened
dowager of passions, shade us from where these plastic pictures arrive
dark appendages connected to suns, by a vortex of larvae plastic
this undulating egress, banquets of flesh plastic
from the predatory bloom, tummy plastic
into which the plastic yarn of omphalic suppuration dripped, on the little skinned fowl
acquainted plastic voices
sugary weeping that would overflow plastic vessels
a murmuring scoop spreads thick dark plastic crystals
until cleaving plastic divisions
smacking flanks to hang upon a plastic hook
suckers whose venom plastic deciphers climax
risen forests restricted from vision plastic
extravagant organisms with whistling stomach plastic

Office of Strategic Services

like, it's polluted
so many things like
it forgot what

        it polluted
        like it forgot
        to pollute

                so many things, like even what it didn't pollute
                it polluted

                        like it
                        overcame
                        forgot to

pollute more of it
like its tower of human skulls found under
noises, globalization, after all that time

spent forgetting it
what an eyesore
it is

down galvanized, structural steel
stairs from what's not on any map where
a dystopian swan swans and slick

lapping water
licks the tufted grasses of the mound.

Under the Direction of Strategic Services II (Provisional)

clamors of dying, cry of having
leached mind, resolute offence
body of refusal, colorful passions
without belief, or law
not hungry, unbelievable appetite
the name of the the, and of it
water, flowers
audacious wishing, dignity of ape
modesty of accord, born like an egg
for the sun, when it called

Motivating the Saboteur

Enter the crucifix, the worst trial of all, when the day is spent
for a chance to begin, a pesky murder of crows
sends customers running to the vans of strangers again
in the box store parking lot, ruining nights
and resurrecting time, restoring balance, in the gloaming
thanks to the lightness of some things
carried some loads turn so heavy and wide
that help is needed to hoist them, I still hear the warbling voices
of my memory, pouring out a carton of milk
over a magical doll
with no arms or legs, but earrings and beads, a colorful cone
shape, wrapped in a rosary
whose name shall be born, I would learn later
how with hair sensing the static of competing poles
the ancestor leaned back, raising its abdomen to the sky
and took off, leaving strands of silk so
deeply soaked, and moved, I slid the door quietly open
when the sky creatures cleared and clouds parted
the pavement smelled and sirens arrived, and thought
where's my mask [2]

---

[2] The ████'s family is scrupulous in complying with recommended and/or required public safety measures, like wearing a mask.

Personal Motives

but i did not write this

hang on, as much, hope, old companion
is no longer, persist, without it, hide
when it steals, tossed, into the raging
atrocities, it dies as well as it
keeps head above
toes, not to lose sight of it, to watch it, the life-saving
it is hung there, suspended, with outstretched hands, gives
to music, the inspired ditch
birds, leaving the nests
naked wing now

Encouraging Destructiveness

The vinegar of fermented fruits
is good for my bite, tincture of ledum
palustre
thistle
but otherwise I'd apply
tourniquets of dental floss, open wound
suck straight out the poison. Should the bone break
rub comfry into it
and set it with twigs. So staunch the wound with yellow flag
or purple loosestrife. Stitch the wound
just as you do
with boiled flax thread. Boil in oil
the needles and tweezers.
Soothe the wounds in poppy milk. Because if it comes in the swab
to stop the spread
the rest can never happen.
When it comes in the cold dampness of the swab
such healing power, soft and gentle, from cotton farm to factory
And so it arrived in the swab
nothing ever happens. In the boot-slapping dance
music spreads, on violin strings
wooden flutes, a panpipe
hollowed-out mouse bones
and a deer-skin drum
damp people hum whose
night winds on
as the thrush introduces
the nightingale.

Safety Measures

creation, enamored, with creation
the unachievable refusing the achievable, it figures
figures of figures, in the swing of beginnings
there were only hallucinating springs, and instant affection

with a sprout of understanding, a critical bloom
studying itself, branchless animation, living chisels living
to refined song, perception of glimpses
traded juices merrily, some chewable implement

with sticky members, jaws decorated
the stare ascends from the carrion, liberated from its shape
by a pure whoosh of photons, hues forge
and multiplying, it finally sees, prances

boiler of refined hysteria, in milky ways, chief pest
this tumult generating its poverty of recall, surplus of material

rains came, floods, merged diminishments
for which passing thought did this pursue sabotage, merging and remerging

muzzling inumerable sputters, the rain sliced to the marrow
with bleak teeth, as if the object might resent its breed
its cargo rattled, a cup, there was naught but swells
these feckless swells, augmenting the chaos

masking the unpleasant display

Tools, Targets, and Timing

Presence of the swab needs
scabs making news making swabs.
Snag—a fluted wind whistles minus three million ants
in the woodpecker's holes—
Dreams are laid into the curious noses and the
work their way into the throat
nestling there. So said the ape—the polecat paralyzes the frog
to keep it fresh. Chimpanzees—
natural born terrorists. The jingle of healing swabs—
too. So much intrigue—
hard to bear. Dolls are fastened with wings—
seeds of the maple. An ant hauling a chestnut—
husk looks like hedgehogs
scaring the field mice. Near the ruined white box—
old grapes resembling a rodent's
poo dries in the meadow. Poison in the powder spread
across the reindeer moss
is effective—the livelihood was gone.
The ugliest reactions once prosecuted
mistreated in a hall of mirrors—
Quite friendly,
but blind as bats.

More Suggestions for Simple Sabotage

beneath the screen of sunshine one polluted the other plastic better it was completed in the plastic morgue of dimness passed every gauge it blazed plastic into its plastic lane but mentally adrift as in when it had barely found its plastic power it merged and foolishly for as soon as the plastic breeze started to gust out of the tongue plastic wickedness shoved into the mouth never again to portray there was a plastic likeness in the rear of the eyeball the initial glimpse was not naïve given tedium then with the new plastic signage want removed the veils and gluttony ensues shock its stinging plastic smell of what never would ever emerge dispersing the germ in the faltering plastic spring until some surprising spewage lofty and vigorous a bit of boisterous plastic heaving up callouses and tools over and over again like a depressed morning glory a plastic shaving of immense loins an avalanche of metamorphic slag plastic complete with an underground roar its personal recitation the plastic formation hears itself wailing whose plastic emptiness impedes and so it dwindled and merged into the plastic atmosphere like plastic clockwork original daydream in the autumn woods the plastic woods wail for it dirt squanders its plastic awareness every time like curses in tissue in cold darkness plastic endlessly propelling as if the froth of limited emotions at the strewn soul's home on the plastic beach recurs presently

Audiences Can Ruin Propaganda Films by Applauding to Drown the Words of the Speaker, by Coughing Loudly, and by Talking [3]

Underground richness
bound together in large families.
In tribes, claiming authority.
Hold them, still, barely visible

on this revolving grindstone. Slap
some water on it, flip it around
"There are photos," proving what you see
with your eye is not

the true story what
feral thing into my eyes
would you project—what plain site
you balancing *Sun*, always shining

naturally your light will shine on me
great *Sun*—you shining balance
what site do you project
"They claim the young are returning to the mainland

after three thousand years"
on foot, bringing expelled news with them, must be
a grunting tale of human suffering, look—
"A fisherman smiles as he pets the hungry shark

caught on his line, who keeps coming back," surprising nobody—
"Common side effect, this natural drug
in even the smallest conceived tyrant
includes grand delusions—

comedy for timing, tragedy for duration.
A hill of bones, really, I'm alighting on the business section—
"When your green ridge gets stripped
as an augur for metropolitan ethereum

purely an acceptance of belief in eternity
will tomorrow believe your balding dome
after the windmills rise and move
and from the lifespans in the fields of your origin

last ten whole years in their sky tower"
I *do* smear toxic goo
from a tree through my hair
and come away looking like that!

made small families, hid the pictures.
"It is a great day
when fresh deposits from space are found
like dust on the ice around the southern pole

"spice for the morning, before accidents, all migratory birds
with the swipe of a pen at eleven to lose
a protected status over the operating cost
of waking up and realizing our dump is full [4]

[3] On the eve of the 50th Earth Day anniversary, a scandalous documentary, *Planet of the Humans*, appears on the Interwebs, produced by a well-known, liberal American firebrand. It's a provocative, Malthusian attack on the sacred cows of Green technology—wind, solar, and biomass—framing them as resource-intensive industries of planet-killing proportions, incapable of sustainably meeting the ever-growing energy demands of an anthropocene. It comes on the heels of a devastating study published earlier in the year, in the open-access *Energy Strategy Reviews* ("An overview of solar photovoltaic panels' end-of-life material recycling," Md. Shahariar Chowdhury et al.), that estimates photovoltaic panel waste will exceed total generation capacity by 2060. Despite the accelerating rate of change within the global climate and the deleterious effects this is having on consumer lifestyles, such dire warnings ironically slide right off the Teflon aspiration invigorating a new marketplace. With such foreboding in mind, the poem references newspaper.

[4] The ▮▮▮▮, stealing George Oppen, an American poet, scribbles this *ars poetica* in the margins:

> A famous poet says, with his fickle hole,
> "poetry is timing."
> No. Comedy is timing
> and tragedy is its duration.
> For the problem is,
> how does one handle filth?

General Interference with Organizations and Production

the object objects to thee
unconvinced, after the plague
all but one property votes
new fence
#biggerpictures
and now here is every body
mindful in the swabbed space
of a pyramid
where waste wastes the time
of others to see
over the foggy cooler aisle
the brightest
upper atmospheres
#biggerpictures
for once
the murder of crows clears, the shoppers
acting surprised and seeming
offended, these excesses
it happens you know
excess excesses excessively
so
#biggerpictures

Other Devices for Lowering Morale and Creating Confusion

in its rout, initiated, this alternative feature of custom
if it's equipped it's unintended, determining naught
had previously been grasped, as though morale
with an indifferent aura, gesticulating original traditions

attempting to muzzle the wail, fixed on its image
after we witnessed the squatting shape, in a deluge of translucent reason
discharging its effluent, beholding its emanation
until sight burst, the ascendent heat expands
enters casually, moves up the nose

dissipates into atmosphere, mutates into a monument of gas
and slipped from the husk, the principal replanted, impatient
until it dispersed again, and being seen now, in the haze needed another
to peel it back, this degradation, propelled by vulgar wants

pitiful, commanded, by treatments, ruin evolved into
a reservoir of hope, feelings unearthed, inside it
until it was monstrously innocent, was impressionable, initially
it knew it in its patterns, but a wail overtook it

Managers and Supervisors

watching
                              a hustle, the sky falls
            the wind

            , these windy
                    conditions, no
floods, inferno
                    shock, wave

            noise
bees   don't notice
            porches

            , along the street
      the lavender sprouts
                        no noise
                        bee response

                        to what
disturbs it what
            breezes pass

      over what's browning and sharp
                with its capsules, the conker tree frees
a dead limb

, in lavender it

      black eyed susan

bounces

spreads

in a puff

Employees

one of the oldest beings *a castle that sits*
at the bottom of a sea *in a fairy tale*
orbits the sun *while a hundred years*
after their first *aerial flight*
the craft's broadcast *location brings back*
small pieces *behind the heat shield, a parachute opened*
while its missing *pre-programmed, experimental, spent seventeen hours jumping*
around, in a crater *it had blasted for this purpose*
but defying this space, now *this simplistic eddy surrounding their sun*
whose forgettable surface, like what core binds their seas, is but molten
I have found the beach, and left it, my own gas
sprays on, solid as a rock, to play my record, for whatever
finds me, in this vast ocean

while under a miscrope *the tiniest bits of a dead star's suds*
cooled and stunning, brought more evidence to their eyes [5]

---

[5] In late 2020, a remnant of Japan's Hayabusa2 ("Falcon") spacecraft returns to Earth carrying a pinch of dust from Ryugu, the "Dragon's Palace." From this, more knowledge will grow.

Automobiles in Quarantine

a pandemic memoir

1,064,572
61,669
4/30
in the year of the pandemic

4/20/2020

A Descent into the President [1]

a m w o n d e r h e a r s e e w a n t a m p r e t e n d f e e l t o u c h w o r r y c r y a m u n d e r s t
a n d s a y d r e a m t r y h o p e a m :

"a m a m a m a m a m a m a m a m a m a m a m a m a m a m a m a m a m a m a m a m a m a m a m a m
a m a m a m a m a m a m a m a m a m a m a m a m a m a m a m a m a m a m a m a m a m a m a m a m a
m a m a m a m a m a m a m a m a m a m a m a m a m a m a m a m a m a m a m a m a m a m a m a m a m
a m a m a m a m a m a m a m a m a m a m a m a m a m a m a m a m a m a m a m a m a m a m a m a m a
m a m a m a m a m a m a m a m a m a m a m a m a m a m a m a m a m a m a m a m a m a m a m a m a m
a m a m a m a m a m a m a m a m a m a m a m a m a m a m a m a m a m a m a m a m a m a m a m a m a
m a m a m a m a m a m a m a m a m a m a m a m a m a m a m a m a m a m a m a m a m a m a m a m a m
a m a m a m a m a m a m a m a m a m a m a m a m a m a m a m a m a m a m a m a m a m a m a m a m a
m a m a m a m a m a m a m a m a m a m a m a m a m a m a m a m a m a m a m a m a m a m a m a m a m
a

---

[1] Because of the novel coranvirus's phenomenal ability to spread and kill, March through April of 2020 sees all but five American states, in the heart of its Midwest, fall like dominoes as governors from both political parties issue lockdown orders that close school buildings, freeze public services, and suspend commerce. Speaking at a presser, an unprepared, filthy rich, plutocratic, orange-colored president protests, "it's my first national crisis, ok?"

4/21/2020 [2]
(societal tones jam) (overheard)

Our covid-19 ain't for free not
Just anyone should have it from me I
hear to work we's s'posed to report you
Musta built yourself a big ole fort for
When you call us in to work today I'm
Lookin' straight your way. Ain't nuttin you can do ain't
nuttin you can say. Our covid-19 ain't for free you
Don't seem worried, you don't seem stressed question all these white studies eat small, cold cigarettes? Death, life, exhaustion? Cognitive dissonance? Where is the mask? Why doesn't the cigarette work? Grow [cough] under recycled rain? Spread it out? Doors eat? Lace your shoes? Why doesn't she walk? Slums, eh? Ah, desolation? Ooh, work? Walk? Shop calmly, like a hot worker? Work, love, life? Where is my bartender, stool? What mask can mask dust, streets? The old hoodie still uses trucks? All men desire dark, old trucks? No fear? No mercy? Lights work? Action is a dented hood? Broken glass? Lights, camera, shop? The shiny street quietly [cough] the vehicle? Streets shop? Masks drive like jackhammers? Hoodies work like dents in the rain? Holes? Anger is a grimy worker? *the streets are emptied and quiet*
but the statehouse, partly cloudy, is on the news
in hoodies, packing the steps, and someone is shooting up boarded-up stores
like they were schools
it's too quiet

---

[2] Protesting the public safety measures adopted by American states to stop the spread of the virus, armed supporters of an orange-colored president crowd the steps of the capitol in Lansing, Michigan. The ball caps and hoodies of a mostly unmasked congregation, donning sunglasses, (skull-masks of the Atomwaffen Division can be seen, under shielded eyes) are there to refuse their duly elected governor's lockdown orders. Later in October the Federal Bureau of Investigation (FBI) foils a plot to kidnap her.

4/22/2020 [3]
the great awakening isolated, social-distance style
"safety has to be dominated"

A night flamed up on fourteen necks. For most of fourteen nights
I sat up, scared time had sunk like bad bread, still setting the alarm.
The nightmares were like works, and works that transubstantiated—callous, novel
In a valley, its Libertarians tore at something before me with a cattle prod.
A night flamed up on fourteen necks and, as if to be cured by some fresh air, somewhere
The uber-individual marched, the red-capped glut of infantry stood their ground—
For the con-tracting of the lung-suck of weakness from these blue-lipped graves
                                        yes from *those* blue waves
Ear, shell, portal, disconnecting, not cooperating, online, memory, sunshine
When some endolymph freaked in the waves of the inner tubes and blockaded the hospital
Jesus Murphy, give this a minute—anonymous masks in honest scrubs oxygenate the street
Diverting the smoggy, vehicular assault last spotted in Charlottesville—and I would give
I would give, I would give, I would give
they said nothing, Give my own red, red mornings like my morgue, overflowing
To the working meek, here there and everywhere muted, inheriting nothing
But the lone heroes, rolling to nowhere in the hairy knuckles of space
Despite dry savory American science and with wet sweet angelic meplat, slogans and flags *Piss off!*
where you from! as if the pure product of the NRA, in the splatter and Styrofoam, the smog, created
Whereas Jonny's poor plague of spiders shan't rise
From the pits of boneheads, whereas my sure redeemer art where the antiseptic wind blows
Whereas human propensity for misery in a fog of dust, blown so my grandfather's young name
Holding their hand, be changed to Milton, whereas this mob of knowing sinners astride, burning pits
Mangled reflections in their fishy shades, automatic weapons, shucked verses, false flags aplenty
Whereas all this so some able-bodied memers of e-doggerel and digital transfer, memorabilia
In the garage, immaculate dentitions so, just—whereas Jonny's spiders when the wind is westerly—
Can hasten to sea on webs loaded with progressive bugs, a world's bedazzled kites.

All trucks shall be flagged as Aryan, groped and searched by hand. Bombs, and behind such tired ears
some years, jokes, and a taciturn Weaver burying the fam in the pellets of their brain food—
Under the old home on the mountain where a liberated road went, dirt, trapped in some pines
Steep cliffs and rivers
Maintained by the words of verses lying, with bodies. Immediately perceives it and feels
When it's touching, demanding wings.

---

[3] Automotive caravans clog the streets of American cities, targeting empty capitol buildings and packed hospitals, but images of nurses standing in the intersections of Denver, Colorado to enforce traffic lights circulate on social media and the evening news, disrupting Operation Gridlock. Tensions are high; everyone knows, and fears, now, how quickly the humble car turns into a weapon, after each "tiki torch incident" caught on phone since Charlottesville, Virginia. Meanwhile, an orange-colored, knowingly despotic president, who supports Gridlock, announces "safety has to predominate" into a microphone at one of his superspreader campaign events. The ██████, listening, at home, is psychologically unprepared to hear this orange-colored mouth correctly pronounce and deploy precise words and, in a fit of understandable misprision, hears the quotation given.

Whitman is trending [4]
Yolo Cruelest Month 2020

Oh, courage!
Multitudes fall!

Ah, adventure!
Oh, desolation!
Oh, courage!

Moons travel!
Mainlands grow!
Gulls fall!
Oh, courage!

Captains fall!
Ah, adventure!

Pirates wave!

Oh, desolation!
Oh, courage!

Moon travel!

---

[4] For some reason, Walt Whitman, another American poet, has a moment in April. Amidst lockdown, virtuality takes over. Shelves grow scarce. Food lines grow. Toilet paper cannot be found. Disinfectant wipes turn good as gold on Ebay.

4/29/2020 [5]
Coleridge celebrity show @YouTube

The reef makes waves like an old thing? *Adventure*
makes a big seashell! Adventure makes a rough reef?
The lively wind swiftly pulls the thing. Moons travel!

Stormy, stormy things quietly lead a big, old wind?
The wave waves like a lively reef!
Never love a thing!

Pirates wave? *Oh, desolation!*
Mainlands grow? *Rise ghostly like a small thing!*
Gulls fall!

The warm cloud roughly views the wind. Never
electrify a sea? *Lively, rough waves quietly lead a rainy, dead mainland.*
Never desire a sail?

Oh, courage!
Endure quietly like a big breeze.
Endurance, endurance, and life!

Where is the rough wind? *Captains fall!*
Ah, adventure!

The misty reef quietly commands the sail.

2/23/2020-5/24/2020

[…]

names…

[…]

A foot on the nail in spring losing to winter's coming heat…

[…]

names…

[…]

Hard skulls relinquishing footwear there, when days following them lighted outside to the clog that fells trees, hating their fancy duds…

[…]

names…

[…]

In the birds' short-lived abundance, around each noplace city, forgetting the booted foot…

[…]

names…

[...]

of cold metal biting into health, the trinkets, burning bridges, feet, stopping the mob in the swamp...

[...]

names...

[...]

5/25/2020 [6]

February 23.
Like rot, this visibility accelerates.
Something else is blossoming.
"spring has been canceled in Georgia."

---

[6] George Floyd is murdered by Officer Derek Chauvin in Minneapolis, Minnesota (USA). Demonstrations will take place across the country and the world, including twenty-three cities in Georgia where, two months earlier, on February 23, two white men in a pickup truck and one in another, who records it, stalk and shoot Ahmaud Arbery, who is out jogging.

5/26-28/2020 [7]
Variational Option Discovery Apps
(more societal tones jam) (overheard)

---

[7] As millions march and millions more shocked Americans stay home, with nowhere to go, watching their own personal interior conflagrations and a global pandemic rages, a maskless, thug-like, orange-colored president also rages, on social media.

5/28-29/2020 [8]

"essential workers"

"the anti-social distance"

---

[8] An unmasked, orange-colored, weak American president signs an order curbing the ability of social media companies to censor fascist propaganda on their websites, but it has no teeth. Later that day, he explains, in his bizarre manner, to an unmasked crowd of thousands, how generosity is actually oppression in disguise, and that American media's "fake news" coverage of new polls showing the public's overwhelmingly negative opinion of last month's Operation America Strong guarantees more towns and cities their own fighter jet displays. I am sorry for these long sentences, but, you know, this revival shit, now, at a time like this, is warped.

5/15/2020

¡el niño del presidente lol un burro habla de las orejas!

tweet "*The chips are starting to crumble! These are truly bad people…*" the chips are starting to crumble! "*The chips are starting to crumble! These are truly bad people…*" no use crying over pissed milk! "*The chips are starting to crumble! These are truly bad people…*" you know what they say! the bigger they are, the more the eggs in the basket flock together! "*The chips are starting to crumble! These are truly bad people…*" how the turns have tabled! "*The chips are starting to crumble! These are truly bad people…*" the tiger is now truly out of the barn! "*The chips are starting to crumble! These are truly bad people…*" down is away and up is far fetched! "*The chips are starting to crumble! These are truly bad people…*" time to shit or get out of the kitchen! "*The chips are starting to crumble! These are truly bad people…*" listen! he's between an alligator and a hard place! "*The chips are starting to crumble! These are truly bad people…*" the chips are starting to crumble! "*The chips are starting to crumble! These are truly bad people…*" it's collapsing like a house of cookies! "*The chips are starting to crumble! These are truly bad people…*" yeah, well, people will do crazy things when the cookies are down! "*The chips are starting to crumble! These are truly bad people…*" i know these concepts are complicated! but chips fall and cookies crumble! "*The chips are starting to crumble! These are truly bad people…*" the cat's out of the cradle, sir! "*The chips are starting to crumble! These are truly bad people…*" looks like the domino's on the other foot! "*The chips are starting to crumble! These are truly bad people…*" the cheese is starting to curl! the milk is starting to jump! the bake is starting to gum! "*The chips are starting to crumble! These are truly bad people…*" people in glass houses sink ships! old dogs are hoisted on new petards! "*The chips are starting to crumble! These are truly bad people…*" cookies crumble and chirps fall, dummy!

6/1/2020 [9]
Variational Option Discovery Apps
(more societal tones jam) (overheard)

Thank him for the flyover—very majestic
Later the night's a bit of vivid blue—
Right now, your nursing homes need the National Guard

---

[9] A choice by the governor of New York State (USA) to sequester elderly COVID-19 patients in nursing homes instead of hospitals creates a horror show. He points somewhere for cause but, unfortunately for him, has been caught wearing nipple rings.

Data Befall Alibi

Data Befall Alibi

Poetry speaks more to the sicknesses
in being. Even if of the poets life is still the
most solicitous. It is not to
dissatisfy anyone. More visitors come here,
that's true. Among me visitors, and a weakness for
the stray. We push it by pure wish and conscience of a
certain risk. My door was never provided with
a doorbell. Recognizable from a distance, at least I hope for it, because I have had a heart
valve for the hospitality which submits to
no law. Huge or cramped according
to mood.
Paradoxically, fortified, transparent. Weak, but
holding out. Displayed in
any weather. This foregttable footprint, it has been
so home, masks and holes, that it became
and the whole mist
was taken. History, this practical joker, ingested in
another way. My peeling destiny should have been to be a textbook, a lead
one probably. I would have been able to not go
to school. It is necessary to know how to
manhandle myths. Let me just say that we took
this, incidentally.
To tease. To whom.
I had borrowed what they lent. Brief like
them. Poetry was only the way
among others.

A Balable Fad I Lit

i borrowed what it lent

What will be amplitude always
of me coming from me in
the heave I divine to toss
my small craft the spaces and I
have time to call the wind I
am reassured No voyage in perspective
the languid clouds touching lightly gently
of steel that one Here is the second
grief? Bird of morning
One loon encouraged by the sunny spell
Here is already the first bird

Baa Data Bill Life

As he is strong this child in these
dangerous games of adults what does
he come to make opening the show why
him he doubts nothing suspects notices
much he speaks little as the
squares of his meals he draws it from
gestures reassured
between good and evil the boundary comes
the call to see into the near future under
the sun he wakes up and lies
down and on every passerby's face he
knows to put a name the streets of his
memory he knows as his pocket as he is
strong this child in no way frightened his
doey eyes open on us his plastic boots that
go up to his knees his shorts blotted with
blood under the shirt of linen the child is there

A Bad Leaf (Lit Bail)

the coffee fills with witnesses, windows and people, all around me
I pause and think hard, familiar element, must it happen
if I raise it to write *to heal with the rust*
from a blade inflicting a wound makes me think [1]
in the middle of the pages, where the cup is put down
absolutely rickety, on the table
a start is needed, if I blow on it, how
will I hear its singing, here is the beach with its opposite bank
about which I know nothing, confusion is in me
big, so much I've enjoyed it, grown small

and I have already drunk my coffee, the coffee is deserted
that nobody fixed me, and me here exact in the rendez-vous

---

[1] A form of magic, it can be used to heal wounds. Nonetheless, a white page, looking south to the American Rust Belt, seems indifferent.

A Balable Fad Lit Bit Lib Tail

read today.

And to be told by tales, angles, a frame, plenty for me
not for fields as far as the eye can see, not for mountains
I ask neither for the sea, honorable pasture
a slice of sky, a breeze, to nibble the eyes
as in a child's drawings, raised by a chimney that smokes
for an old house's hovels in the background
which I refuse to reconsider, several trees
and more important, paths
personas and plugs, flags and strange odors, lit squares of grass, doors with a view
how to the right arm, one day, arthritic decor abruptly changed
I do not have to complain, through the screen, you see it
up to aphasia, hostilities, that I must declare myself to it
the line for a unique seat, through the pissy stacks, to the parsimonious hashtag of joy
in view of all manner of cats, debris, yards, fibrous and rusty
the lack of comfort, I accept isolation
I stay there, I am there
I desert it, here is therefore the home which lives in me

Bail

are you there, nameless, oh
nameless, when the setting is still lacking
a harness only, there are the rooms

manhandled by subjacent ironies, they
remain fragile, as for questionings
each fall is so bearable, something become

established, to be climate
for a handful of notes, buried rhythm
harnesses, laws, how books began

Reports

                                        spreading meat
                                    lines as they waited
                                    incorruptible wind

                                        inexhaustible
                                    from the crowd
                                    in the blanched air

                                        and new convection
                                    on this earth

That homicidal bird impaling them on thorns and barbed wire
aggressive is this dumb bird begging
That dopey legged raptor's a fraud with carrion
and this one's the worst stashing garbage for shame
Eating later one morning wake up
to all that stupid singing realize
Canada went South [1]

---

[1] The ████ discovers the joys of birding during his family's second mandatory quarantine following exposure to Americans infected with COVID-19, just twenty miles from the Canadian border, then closed.

the sun fell
into a lamp
the sun fell

into coffee
into food
the sun fell

the sun fell
into the street
into sentences

the sun fell
into colorful worms
into cellulose and water

and a plague
the sun fell
the sun

fell
and could not get up
the sun fell

into fields
the sun fell
passed windows

the sun fell
on my parts
on a big outing

the sun fell
with the rain

en c ul t u r at e d en c ul t u r at e d en c ul t u r at e d en c ul t u r at e d en c ul t u r at e d

      where
      afterwards
         appear
     causing

      meaningful
      relations

        afterwards
        appear
        causing
        where

      meaningful
      relations

        appear
        causing
        where
        afterwards

      meaningful
      relations

        causing
        where
        afterwards
        appear

The parts of our bodies traceable to stars preying on them in their cores
Spewing these enriched ingredients pooping across the galaxy, a long time ago for
Such reasons connected to earth, and connected
To a universe, we are dust, the parasites flushed for whom
Things then exist by designation

The closest living relative to Tyrannosaurus Rex is a chicken, birds kept as pets like doves, parakeets, lovebirds live naturally in pairs. The smallest bird egg belongs to the hummingbird they're the size of a pea. The largest from the ostrich is a cantaloupe. A bird's eye consumes fifty percent of a bird's head the penguin can swim but not fly, they do walk upright. Owl head swivels in a circle but cannot move their eyes chicken makes two hundred distinct communiqués. When it comes to birds the male has glamorous feathers, coloration songs and dances, female chooses their mate. Documented homosexual and/or transgender behavior in five hundred species as of their dancehall in nineteen ninety-nine. An estimated third of all bird owners leave the radio on for their pets. Reptiles were laying eggs long before chickens appeared. The greasy goose the first domesticated bird. Kiwi birds are blind they hunt by smell. Several breeds of chicken lay colored eggs, like green or blue or brown, the old saying you eat like a bird means you eat like a pig. A gathering of larks being an exaltation, a group of chickens being a peep; a smattering of geese being a gaggle, a swarm of ravens being a conspiracy: the nightmare of owls is parliament. Chickens laying brown eggs have red ear lobes. A genetic link between the two. Crow's largest cerebral hemispheres, mockingbirds can imitate many sounds.

the biggest meat in the ocean approaching peaceful clouds of the tiniest meat in the ocean opening mouths, readying tails, and asking, is it worth it

standing motionless scanning the eddy wading to their belly on long stately legs, they can strike a fish like lightning in flight long legs trailing behind on the way to their partner, *roh-roh-roh* from above, the beacon clucking *go-go-go* building to *frawnk frawnk frawnk* and feeling something a screaming *awk chicks going* tik-tik-tik *within minutes of hatching* in a moment the two will *clapper the fish drops* at each other, chattering tips of the bill

carrying off another meal, one that loved, his or her bloodied feathers I haven't seen me for months, I just climbed on land, though I've dreamt them consecrated them, with unlimited means songbirds shooting one, now tell me cooler in front

(

plastic sheets (windows
things of the past

absorbent butcher block
on top of the earth

(

in the key of spring

as a squiggly green line developed a crisp tall peak the will to fly is strong in this one just climbed on land as twenty percent less matter than should be *was contained* in the largest known structure ever spotted *a colder part of space* missing ten thousand galaxies *named* catechesis buckled a shunt *a parallel universe bumps into our own like nothing and we like* nothing? *just balloon up like trillions of others?* big bang I say shoot first die last stay low move fast one shot one kill no luck pure skill hallelujah hosana jah yah al shokr le allah maranatha amen [2]

---

[2] Evidence mounts that friction with an adjacent universe, not too far from us, a mere three billion light-years, apparently, accounts for the abonormally cold region of space, a fluctuation in the Cosmic Microwave Background, the so-called "afterglow of creation," repeatedly measured by astronomers in Australia, England, Finland, and the U.S. between 2010 and 2017. Missing tens of thousands of solar systems and galaxies that should otherwise be there, the ███ still believes he has read that mathematical models predicting the existence of a multiverse are increasingly used to explain such anomalous voids in the distribution of astral phenomena. (The hunt is on for gravitational ripples whipped up by continuous interference of perpetual objects passing through—"inflation," ultimately producing new Big Bangs.)

                                        / the future gains
                                        / no knowing
                                        / no point
                                        / repeating myself

            next door turned sick / desire is complacent
            seemed interesting tho / in front of the question
                    we got soaked / where the ends
                        good money / ignoring

                    multiplying flag / the foam
                out there / stuck to the riverbed
        pure superfund country water / indigenous now

                                        / accustomed to flying
                                        / right through it
                                        / over contaminated ground

                        surly / where all take in
                    as ma bypassin / with vision
                Transit / a creek ran through it

Lawns, angelic foundations, birds formed with the seeds feet trampled, in the flesh of sour
worms. Their revelation doesn't comfort me, out of kindness, their meat is what's been denied.
Infernal, snake dens, traceless for overnight activity, the spoiled blossoms of the years, the fleshy
blockages of the drought, of the sun's raw power, the skinned exhibitions of humble days, the
least fraudulent antonyms of what unfortunate light has been found, what diurnal chattering,

what sorrow of starlight, of quiet waiting, not for dark, bleak vision. Flesh yet immortal, in light of the greased visions of the animals, would listen to those least mechanical abstractions, to painful dirt, being joyful, ignoring and knowing the simplifying mask of denial, those birdfeeders covered in birdshit.

shared
grace
chlorinated
border
spotted
food
painful
freedom
sucker
dumpster
shared
bad
memory

Just north of somewhere, [3] a rare cream recently reappeared. Experts say it consists of salt, household chemicals, plant matters, fish decomposition, unknown excretions from seaweed—a frothy gathering of oceanic currents. Pushed toward land, a windy turbulence whipped it up so thick that a blanket of it claimed an island's eastern-facing beaches for three days. One resident, who wishes to remain anonymous, explained, *it was quite cool to touch and it was really weird. It was like clouds of air—you could hardly feel it.* Others, also asking for anonymity, recalling, *me and my mates just spent the afternoon leaping about in that stuff.* No adverse health effects have so far been reported.

---

[3] Too little is known about the cream's origins. Privacy is required (to protect tourists).

European Great Tits in hollow trees bludgeoning roosts of bats to death before dragging them out to eat the bats having their heads pecked open. The live flesh of the Giant Right Whale seen leaving in the Kelp Gull whose population growth is blamed on human waste. The European White Stork unhappy with their meals running away from parents to the neighbors. Iron Hornbills shaping barriers of mud shit and sticks around the females and the young through which the male is passing frogs mice and fruit imprisoning his family until they fledge. The Palm Cockatoo with their *Mohawk* beating the breeding hollow he has to show like a drum with a branch like a broom handle snapping in a hooked bill. Tiger Herons Pittas Hawks and Egrets crashing to the ground in dramatic and unexplained confusing state. The House Wren defending territory preferred by insects doesn't *ruin competing nests* when males hell bent on eradicating entire families require but small pecks while building his own target. While most birds are fucking in a hollowed out tree on a branch or public sandbar relatives of Whippoor Wills and Hummingbirds known as Swifts crossing continents in three days colliding at two hundred miles per hour two thousand feet in the air fucking faster than aircraft are launching but having trouble perching. Red-breasted Nuthatches glopping toxic conifer goo around their nest. Tawny Frogmouth perfectly resembling a dead branch waiting for birds frogs and lizards flies to enter swallowing hole the click echoing a hundred feet away.

what's the use anyway
like flies the young
squirm (and sprouts wings
born of a heaven) pride of the female
fear of the male (down there
it's happening) they seem to know this
they push it (amongst it
bodies circulate) out, never across
only out

In tree branches somewhere, a brood of strange nymphs hatch, fall, and burrow into the ground. For the next seventeen years they'll feed on sap from the roots of their natal trunks. They'll need to transform five times before tunneling back to the surface, where on a midsummer day the largest migration on the planet sluggishly appears. It emerges from soil, cascading back up into the canopy, where they transform one last time. Young, but old, slow, and many, soon the woods' inhabitants are gorging themselves on these elderly, winged babies who mate, lay eggs, and die. There are far too many to stomach and, that summer, a spongy carpet of decomposing bodies will rise from the forest floor, whose eggs are now wriggling in the trees. Periodical cicadas are tactical, practicing what science calls *predator satiation*. In the years that they die, experts say tree rings record visible growth spurts.

even considering (king goat
is skittering spray) as not not belonging (losing
rope for its reign) does not guarantee
(only silhouettes last)
the transmission of character needed (no one
remembers the names
of well-wishers
time halts the arc of a missile) to keep a low
profile

All matter together explaining and administering material conditions required for life, their Earth resembling a giant, self-regulating organism, post-human in nature, seaming something more useful than proven, (indeed!) as reification of Organ is umm presenting plausible paths to the mass of acceptance in thoughts requiring transcendences of the Abrahamic individualisms weaving the global consumption of human is umm dead phase through environmental precarity (indeed!)

All attempts to define Organ is umm positing life and their features as emerging in spontaneous increments from random, increasingly complex patterning, spontaneous organization, (indeed!) the emergent appearing of life in their accelerating features antithetical to a mechanistic, Newtonian explication of life producing linear causes and effects, the boggy conditions (indeed!) suffocating untraceable phemonana demanding a scholarly upheaval in the way author-ities (unlike this ▮▮▮▮) choose to not blame unproven environmental pollutants (indeed!)

* (indeed!)

* (indeed!)

* (indeed!)

a driven river flew the big humming bird
in its annual passing had nothing to do with it
never thought this was in the mountains splayed

a mystery like a cloud shades opposite bank
a day is reporting a brain is perched
their own sorry names watching lucky heads

drawn to what could wish all terrains vehicles
to live more intensely emptied and silent
no rattle rattles imaginary known

flags become real remains yet imaginary
as orange ants were biting blinded like visions
the endless divisions ever diminishing visions

on the way into what was there to say
shrinking mountains under that boot

"Thursday morning a squiggly green line developed a crisp, tall peak. The external source should have called home, during the plunge, this passage had had every confidence. It actually had happened last night, but had it breached protocol and even reached a waiting audience of friends and family in time…evening came with little reason to doubt the external source would call home but it couldn't help my nerves, this was all still the beginning of its inevitable death. While the people in the room were proud of sending the old machine to do something new and symbolically rich they struggled with the knowledge of what we were actually doing. The external source was like a member of the family, inextricable from the growth of children." [4]

---

[4] The international Cassini spacecraft marks humanity's longest continuous orbital mission around a heavenly body by surviving an impromptu, mid-summer plunge through the icy rings of Saturn, only to find itself retired somewhere in space.

a second baseman known for their stance
on assimilation and identity, working with leprosy patients
develops a cure for the disease, a doctor who suggested

network of picturesque nasal chains
of linear time through orifices everywhere elevators
open and filter like
sovereign consumption of an ad

an asteroid precipitates the extinction of dinosaurs
writing a medical column and launching a product line
in the frozen food section, a model and designer

untranscended and opaque swimming
in self-evident truths porous
news wafts
in social space generated immanently

launching a lifestyle website, turned independent filmmaker
cum military language and culture consultant,
a director of character and content development

on the wind on the air
a shard of real tissue selves and others
made up
of common tastes

a world renowned war correspondent
and news anchor, turns to churches
bringing converts into governance

From the nests in the eaves of Earth, oh

Your mild poop crowning the clever dancers of May!

Good luck!

a multi-pronged event to overhaul
shopping meat work grinder school meat
body grinder raids has you sleeping until noon
or whenever it suits you /
anyone who experiences problems
has been urged to report it so
forget the alarm /
so breathe deeply / so love and love and love and love /
love! it is scheduled to last
many days

Acknowledgments

Poems from this manuscript were first published in *Blazing Stadium, Dispatches from the Poetry Wars, E-ratio, Unlikely Stories Mark V,* and in the chapbook *Needles of Itching Feathers* (The Operating System). "Infection" was self-published and distributed under a pseudonym.

About the Author

Jared Schickling's poems, essays, and interviews have appeared in many journals, some now defunct, including *Interim; Marsh Hawk Review; 1913: a journal of forms; Drunken Boat; Bombay Gin; Ecopoetics; Exquisite Corpse; Cordite Poetry Review; Bookslut; Literary Imagination; The Café Review; Posit; Borderlands: Texas Poetry Review; Big Bridge; Jacket; Jacket2; Little Red Leaves; Poetry Northwest; Word For/Word: a journal of new writing;* and anthologized in *The End of the World Project Anthology* (Moria Books) and *Resist Much/ Obey Little: Inaugural Poems to the Resistance* (Dispatches Editions/Spuyten Duyvil). He is the author of several poetry books and chapbooks. He edited *A Lyrebird: Selected Poems of Michael Farrell* (Blazevox, 2017), and for some years edited a freely distributed, international mimeo-zine, *eccolinguistics*. He  has worked in various editorial capacities for Alice James Books; Tarpaulin Sky; the Center for Literary Publishing at Colorado State University; New American Press and *Mayday Magazine; Reconfigurations: A Journal for Poetics and Poetry / Literature and Culture;* and behind the scenes for the recent *Poetics for the More-than-Human World: An Anthology of Poetry and Commentary* (Dispatches Editions/Spuyten Duyvil). He teaches English in Buffalo Public Schools, and edits Delete Press and The Mute Canary, publishers of poetry.

Other Books by Jared Schickling

For Love (the order of the echoes) (Blazevox Books, 2020)

Guides, Translators, Assistants, Porters: a polyvocal American epic minus the details (2018)

Needles of Itching Feathers (The Operating System, 2018)

The Mercury Poem (Blazevox, 2017)

Donald Trump in North Korea (Moria Books' Locofo Chaps, 2017)

Donald Trump and the Pocket Oracle (2017)

Province of Numb Errs (Blazevox, 2016)

The Paranoid Reader: Essays, 2006-2012 (Furniture Press, 2014)

Two Books on the Gas: Above the Shale and Achieved by Kissing (Blazevox, 2014)

ATBOALGFPOPASASBIFL: Irritations, Excrement and Wipes (2013)

Prospectus for a Stage (LRL Textile Series, 2013)

A Packet of Food, in *Omnia Vanitas Review: A Journal of Literary Erotica 2* (2013)

The Pink (Blazevox, 2012)

t&u& lash your nipples to a post history is gorgeous (2011)

Zero's Blooming Excursion (2010)

O (2009)

Submissions (2008)

Aurora (2007)

Suburban Eggs (self-published, 2003)

Recent Titles from Unlikely Books

Here, Which Is Also a Place by Mark DuCharme

White Van by Meg Tuite

Flight Advice: a fabulary by Tobey Hiller

A Brief Conversation with Consciousness by Marc Vincenz

~getting away with everything by Vincent A. Cellucci and Christopher Shipman

fata morgana by Joel Chace

Typescenes by Rodney A. Brown

Political AF: A Rage Collection by Tara Campbell

The Deepest Part of Dark by Anne Elezabeth Pluto

Swimming Home by Kayla Rodney

Manything by dan raphael

Citizen Relent by Jeff Weddle

The Mercy of Traffic by Wendy Taylor Carlisle

Cantos Poesia by David E. Matthews

Left Hand Dharma: New and Selected Poems by Belinda Subraman

Apocalyptics by C. Derick Varn

Pachuco Skull with Sombrero: Los Angeles, 1970 by Lawrence Welsh

Monolith by Anne McMillen (Second Edition)

When Red Blood Cells Leak by Anne McMillen (Second Edition)

My Hands Were Clean by Tom Bradley (Second Edition)

anonymous gun. by Kurtice Kucheman (Second Edition)

Soy solo palabras but wish to be a city by Leon De la Rósa, illustrated by Gui.ra.ga7 (Second Edition)

www.ingramcontent.com/pod-product-compliance
Lightning Source LLC
Chambersburg PA
CBHW080847120626
46553CB00009B/2613